How do you like our book?

We would really appreciate you leaving us a review.

Other Picture Books:

For other fun Picture Books by Kampelstone,
simply search for:

Kampelstone Picture Books 🔍

Facts about Golden Retrievers

- Of 196 dogs on the American Kennel Club's list, Golden Retrievers rank third on the list of most popular dogs in the USA after Labrador Retrievers and German Shepherds.

- Presidents Ford and Reagan both had Golden Retrievers during their presidencies.

- Goldens are known to take care of other animals, even cats.

- Golden retrievers are loving and caring dogs. They are very good dogs for a family. In a study of thirty dog breeds, Goldens were found to be the least aggressive.

- Golden Retrievers Are excellent therapy dogs. They can soothe and calm people and seem to have high empathy and unconditional love for people.

- If left alone for more than about seven hours Goldens can become sad and lonely.

- As natural athletes, they're always ready to engage in active play whether it's a game of fetch, hiking, swimming, or other exercise. However, this characteristic prevents them from being good guard dogs. They're apt to want to simply play with whoever shows up.

  The average lifespan of Golden Retriever is 12-14 years

- They are considered full grown at about one year old and the adult dogs typically weigh between 55 and 75 lb (25 and 34 kg).

- Originally bred as dogs to assist hunters, they instinctively love to swim. They're always up for a game of fetch at the beach or at a lake. Two characteristics which help them swim is that they have water-repellent double coats and that they have webbed toes.

- They are hard-working and easy to train which makes them popular as "actors" in Movies and TV shows.

- Golden Retrievers are the 4th smartest dog breed behind Border Collies, Poodles, and German Shepherds.

- Golden Retrievers are often used on search and rescue teams since they have such a sharp ability to track. They are also often employed as trackers, hunting and service dogs.

- Golden Retrievers were developed as a breed in Scotland by Lord Tweedmouth in 1868 by breeding a Wavy-coated retriever with a Tweed Water Spaniel

- They love to eat and will eat anything, from the dinner in their bowl to toys, paper, and crayons. They love to eat so much that unless, checked, they can become obese.

- They are at their most active very early in the morning.

- They are capable of running 30 MPH (48 kph).

- Their sense of taste is much less than a human's since they have about 1700 taste buds compared to 9000 in a human. But their sense of smell is likely 100,000 times more keen than a human's.